BEAUTY UNSHAKEN

FARAH ALQATTAN

Words from the Author

Womanhood,

Our franchise is a beauty. Feel not shaken when you have been harmed or taken for granted. This is a token of appreciation to you for all you have been through. Thank you for the days you've poured, not only love, but soul. Feel appreciated for the essence you carry, if you are a woman, part of this legacy.

We hope you enjoy these poems!

BEAUTY UNSHAKEN

Copyright @ 2025 by Farah Alqattan

All rights reserved. No part of this book may be reproduced in any manner whatsoever without written permission, except in the case of brief quotations embodied in articles and reviews.

Print Version: 4, 2025
Print ISBN: 979-8-9881785-6-9
Library of Congress Control Number: 2025903945
For permission or media requests contact: farahalqattan.author@gmail.com
Author Instagram: farahalqattanofficial

Rwh Publishing LLC produces creative content by artists who aim to uplift humanity and change lives for the better.

Table of Contents

Fine Tune ---------- 8
Equanimity ---------- 9
Grid Lock ---------- 10
Spy-der Web ---------- 11
Frequency Reverberates ---------- 13
Seeded Spring ---------- 16
Nurturing Oracle ---------- 17
Jedinstvo ---------- 19
Vita ---------- 22
Fluorescent Returns ---------- 23
Heart and Courage ---------- 25
Compassionate Paragon ---------- 28
Magnetic Affections ---------- 29
Candid Fairness ---------- 31
Account Able ---------- 33
Top Honor ---------- 35
Powerful Dedicates ---------- 36
Higher Velocity ---------- 37
Blindfold Unfolding ---------- 38
Honorable Gentle-Men ---------- 40
Sweet Macaroons ---------- 41
Cortex Cortisol ---------- 43
Stoic Enigma ---------- 44
Fortress Faith ---------- 45
Beautiful and Unshaken ---------- 47

Gold Mine ---------- 49
Connective Patent ---------- 51
Musky Timber ---------- 52
Visual Spectrum ---------- 53
Easy Breezy, Lemon Squeezy ---------- 54
Recognition Ignition ---------- 55
Diamond Wings ---------- 56
No Strings Attached ---------- 57
Lady Liberty ---------- 60
Hope Happenings ---------- 61
Lily Pond ---------- 63
Virtue Exfoliation ---------- 66
Elemental Productions ---------- 66
Unified Faction ---------- 69
Catalyst Conduit ---------- 71
Energy Vibrations ---------- 72
Gracious Discretion ---------- 73
Bright Future ---------- 74
Factorial ---------- 75
Fertile Integrity ---------- 76
Star Spangled Banner ---------- 77
Mountain Peak ---------- 79
Step Up ---------- 80
Orange Tangerines ---------- 82
Beyond Enduring, Endearing ---------- 83
Tennis Love ---------- 85
Together ---------- 87
Withdrawal Reflex ---------- 90
Sweet Pressure ---------- 91
Covered Goodness ---------- 94
Score ---------- 95
Lady Justice ---------- 97

5 ~ FARAH ALQATTAN

Deep Breaths

3

2

1

7 - FARAH ALQATTAN

Fine Tune

For what is an offense?
If it were not of an act and intention

How have emotions affected?
As each moved through experience

Is one able to understand why so many are hurting?

The choice is made,
"We lead with love, doing different"
Leaving a better imprint
Than any who have oppressed generations

Is it pink or purple
Red or blue
Can each rise up to see through?

Accountability
Rather than popularity

Equanimity

Stand tall
Upright
Not in physical weapons
But foundations

What is each standing upon?
Is it understanding from water fountains?

How much has each aimed to learn inner workings?

If you're feeling lost
Find the light
That shines brighter amidst the darkness
Is it a womanhood franchise?

Some tug or suggest
Be it people or products for attention
Ways away misleading

There are others, cheering for you
Sharing a signal like a lighthouse
As an indicator

Not feedback loops
The echo chambers and narratives
Even false statements

Grid Lock

Through the environment and landscapes
What has been repeated?

If not kind expression and natural beauties
As each travels the distance
Notice the common denominators

Who protects and guards?
Not selfish or greedy
Absolves

You can go to the best cities
Then talk to the people, hear complaints
Of the overworking
People not being able to enjoy life given

Where is the joy? Where is it?
Does a beauty have to keep hearing the cries of her neighbors?

Why need a woman as a leader?
When she's got intuition from the heavens
Building a shelter
Or is it ego
How are people seeing her?

Is the glow found yet?
To experience homeness

When nothing was needed to experience luxury
Aside, kind and gentle expressions
Treasures

Spy-der Web

Intercom
That dot com
Cassettes or CDs
Record tapping
Indexing

Oh who is a developer out here?
Can one perceive what has been threaded and woven?

Hospitals or prisons
Be it physical or for reels?
Even algorithms in harmful sites, that propagate womanhood traffic

Oh the hurt can cloud sight and hearing
As each goes about mimicking
Even partying
Or is it tailgating?

Projections and cycles of abuse
While others profit and say we're protectors

Who developed the best?
Tell me who?
If not womanhood franchise, trying to keep the children safe
Until they go to schools that tell them
"It's okay, use a condom it'll protect you"

The energy is not physical
Weaving into your mind, while each operates with others who are inhibited
Halo Effect bias

Frequency Reverberates

We are more than the hurt
We are more than the harm
Empty vases
Left to be broken

We are more
A better franchise
Who will extended farther out, not falling
Or failing
Even flailing out

Wiping the tears
Of those who have been hurting
In beds, since the beginning

How long will they sleep?
While they try to take the best out, not even on a date, complaining

This franchise is about to change the tides
For a better future
"It's totally possible"

Is it this generation or will it take women?
To give life a new beginning

Even with all the popularized materials, making one rationalize different
Each has great inner strength
To not be swayed, reverberating soul expression

If any can perceive
Translate the offering
Not for success or materials
For higher purpose
Leading to the sacred

If you learn the truth
The responsibility required of you
Take accountability and do different
No longer blaming womanhood

15 - FARAH ALQATTAN

Seeded Spring

You were born in a surplus
Don't let experience make you rationalize
In doubt leading to droughts

You are born into a surplus if you can see
How much life is here?
Above land or even underwater
Plentiful, in the moral pocket

Can you pay respect or attention?
It's better to think different, not losing your senses

You know, they're trying to go to mars
Hope they've spent as much time being grateful for what's here

What's the secret sauce
Who has energy activation?
Powers up without fuel tanks
Gets you out of this world into the celestial

Want to get on the shuttle?
Or the ship?
Alright, grip

We're taking off
A new time
Or is it womanhood franchise leading?

Nurturing Oracle

If only each knew
The truth
Beyond mortal expression or inhibitors

If only, each could
Imagine
How each may be guilty even a little bit

The truth would not try to alter
Or set anyone up on an altar

What happened through generations?
Conquers and conquests
Even tyrants

Who lasted beyond the times?
Did any hear the messages?
Immortals

When each is facing a due date
How have nerves and senses taken shape?
A frenzy, amidst the mystery

This is the time to put the past behind
Not to ignore what has happened
Or abandon the lessons
Learning how grief and resentment affect behavior

Is each still bitter? Wiping out
All the goodness of the present moment that poured into their cups
Sweet womanhood franchise

Don't feel as if it is not seen or known
How those manipulators are scheming
The greed is tasty, nothing fulfills it
But if you are a true one, true love will be enough for you

Jedinstvo

What will the investment in spirit essence provide?
Perhaps threading awareness
Not tearing anyone or breaking hearts
Mocking vulnerable past or parts

Who has led in the infrastructure?
Some pick instant gain, not weighing
The aftermath in cities after generations
Is it a crime manifestation?

Why won't any believe
Threading different will do it
Not tricking with manipulation

Who and what pours trueness?
If not breath
When men say, "Don't bite the hand that feeds you"

Who owns the elements, who?
Who created all that is under the sun for mortals to possess and consume?

So breathe so deep
Love is in the air
Perhaps, it's accountability

The truth is all around
It's not even rocket science
But if they could, they'll try to possess it

Spooky spooky, who's a ghost or vampire
Wanting to haunt others and buy blood

21 - FARAH ALQATTAN

<u>*Vita*</u>

Girl, look in the mirror
What do you see?
Is it that true reflection of who you were meant to be?

Are you feeling bent and broken?
Low because of consumption

Look again after reading this
And remember, our imprints are different
Womanhood is sacred

These words will change conscience and mental models
Perhaps wipe that dirt off of her from world operations

The soul is untainted and won't be touched
By the filth
Even with all the marketing exploiting attention
Deceptions

That's it, she knows
She didn't see herself as so
If it wasn't for misperceptions or deceptions tugging at her optics

She takes bravest steps
As she looks again
Standing on this
What does she see?

'Beauty that's unshaken,
deep in the essence of her soul iris'

Fluorescent Returns

Where do the thoughts stem from?
Check your connection

Are any rooted in authenticity?
Or did someone get plugged into other functions
Even with offers of dangled money
You are no donkey

Oh the matrix is about to be so upset
A whole bunch are getting unplugged
Away from destruction

Did any think by design, none were embedded
To put in place those who would try to kill the innocent

This place is glowing different
Can any see?
Souls meant to be glimmering

The mothers and the daughters
Wait, "What about the boys and men?"
Yes, everyone be made honorable on this canvas

Should any choose
Treating with dignity
Clothing insecurities
Armor of acceptance of the making

The dermis not being picked on
Because of the origins of condescends
Not having seen them wholesome

Lift your head dear
Even if you were not comforted since you were a child

Who made you? Perfect in creation
Until you consumed what has been made in the open

You think you are imperfect why?
Wipe those tears because you were never meant to not feel,
as if you are not good enough to breathe

Oh, every mirror will break
For anyone who made you feel or think less than

Know you are made with dignity and worth
Even when you change nothing, we see your beautiful glow

The soul lens won't have anyone lost
In the body function
It'll elevate

Are you ready to take flight?
To no longer be hurting
Or reaching for a scalpel rather than accepting
The design
The glow
Like a bright star in the darkness

Heart and Courage

The fill up from another can have one looking about
In pride and ego

Who lures the best in, so they are not shown how they're already glowing?
Only if each injects or slices parts of themselves to fit in

Who's after that wholesome aura?
Treasured womanhood precious perils

Who is stealing our treasures?

Who took your spark in ownership?
Is it your family? private sector? Or the government?

Emperors
It's getting pathetic

Having to see you cry when it's your birthday
When all you did was bear others through their sickness

Oh you are seen
Not only in the shiny things but hurting

I will grip any from touching you
Unkindly
Their reckoning will come upon them in the morning

True beauty shines like no other
Especially in front of the haters who tried to overpower her

Even misguides with dilutions in operations
For success or profit gains
Look who's waste size is getting bigger
It's a heavy punishment

They're about to find out who really is the worthy one
Womanhood, is it singularity?
"I'm so sorry"
You deserve an apology

Why is anyone with power trying to control her?
Was she not made to roam with sacred quintessence?
Without opinionated blemishes
That tainted perceptions

27 - FARAH ALQATTAN

Compassionate Paragon

Can one help another see?
Better than the lies that the blind feed

Can any see this whole place glowing?
In radiance, each soul deserving
Not falling for illusions
Darkening perceptions

You are safe and secure in your making
Others too
Choose to put down the weapons
Insecurities and transferred false narratives
Hate and gossip

What's your attire?
Even this author knows, the best is being a spiritual warrior

Not sure what that means
Let's explain
It involves no weapons physically perceived
It oozes with kindness and good deeds

"What's a deed?"
It's ancient verbiage for actions
Don't forget, intention makes all the difference

Magnetic Affections

This may be the greatest wealth transfer
If you can perceive, objective

Can you check this out?
The true fortune pouring truth understanding

The greatest wealth transfer, indeed
If only one can perceive, building
To no longer be propagating the hurting

It's going to make billions through generations
Is it money or soul sacred functions
What do each value?

Not all desire is bad
Some passions can lead to blindness, full of emotions
There's a difference, when it's purpose

Oh hear the ceremony
Dings and dongs
Heartbeats beating
Shouting from the mountain tops
"We fail not nor falter.
We will fight forever"

So priceless how kindness can make the difference
When others reach for weapons
She is a healer

It's a thing of beauty
Womanhood lifting higher
Without greed, extinguishing fire

To not ask for a dollar but share an ounce of bread
They try and try to make it artificial
But little do they know the true connection, higher intelligence

So who is winning the war?
It's only projections

What are your decisions based off of?
Is it love or objects?

One frees
While other reel, developing dependency
Rather than empowering to independence, freedom fortune
Omnipresence in sense making
Better perceive who's in the pit, luring you in
When another tries to reach for you to get you out of it

Each will have to bare their ending
And witness what they've propagated

Are you undressing others bare?
Or rising to cover, the sacred womanhood franchise

"This sounds pretty serious"
Indeed it is
Because it's time someone stood up for the innocent

Each is valued and valuable
Each deserves to heal and overcome
Knowing they weren't made less than

Candid Fairness

The day you are in judgment
Perhaps crucified
When others throw dirt on your name
And call you all sorts of things

Hateful energy because you're not listening
When intuition is overpowering all of them, to move you into goodness

They may reject you and say your no good as others
Stay true and speak, "May peace and love be with you"

How quick are we to ostracize
When we have witnessed actions of the goodness before hearing falsehood

Can we reach in our pocket to give out forgiveness and kindness
Paying respect
Warming up the hearts, it's possible

Or is this place morally bankrupt full of luxury and coins
Who has true value?

Expression can change things about you
Muscles of character function
Are you weak or having great strength?

Don't let others behaviors change or taint you
It's not a connective tissue virtue

You have to consciously choose
To see the kindness in others and remember the good that has been poured
Over the tasty resentment that can blind the best from seeing
How much good can come from each of us

Immunity will be a shield
Resilience
Not falling to subjective opinions
Is it soul conditioning?
Enemy forgiveness
You're about to be everyone's favorite person

Account Able

How can each see or perceive?
They made their decision not to believe

Everyone has the opportunity
To choose love
Instead of deciding they knew better than
Womanhood franchise

What's the easiest way to end competition?
If not distracting and distorting generations

Here, take this
Not a clue
But an armor

Choose belief
When others belittle the sacred origins
Womanhood franchise

Believe in the word
Love
And witness immunity expand outwards

Force-field as big as the universe
Even when they're building an iron dome

So be brave to stand up for friends and family
Even in private discussion, separated
Each word carries a frequency

Step up
Step on this
Let yourself attune
With the beautiful and unshaken

Love is irrational
Beyond all things
That's why love like ours
Can do the impossible and win

-smiles-

Top Honor

The author keeps buying journals for logs and documentation
But her soul reaches through with love pouring
Understanding

Through each scene and page
Reminding
"There is more to us.
Don't let the misguided have you think you are made less significant"

She's going to cramp this hand
Writing
"We are so much more than hurtful experiences.
That is a reflection of soul suffocation."

This has got to do it
The will
It's possible
Beating the odds

Was Moses not struck by lightning?
Before he parted the waters to save his people

You have no idea how many clues have been given
For those believers
Rising higher
A vibration of hope
Bright genius minds
Not allowing bruises to be left inside anyone

Powerful Dedicates

They say life is a battle between good and evil
It really isn't
Each started in darkness
Before becoming light-hearted

So let all of you be anomalies
This place is about to glitch in radiance
Temples glowing

Perhaps, it's just an epiphany

Higher Velocity

Even if you're cold or gold
Fat or impure

Even if you're a brunette or blonde
Natural or extraordinary

Even if you're muscular or tweetling thumbs
In a wheelchair or running marathons

Even if you can share your thoughts out loud or silent because of fear
Herald from praises or feeling left out

Even if you're the A+ student or cleaning orchids
A grandma without offspring or butterflies with wings

Even if the worst has happened and the happy ever after is yet to be founded
Making a movie or sharing cupcakes in nurseries

Even if it's one day you're here then have gone there
Through so many experiences

Even if you were to be anything or nothing at all
Know, you have been made for a purpose
This womanhood franchise
Not lacking anything
Having a glowing inner glimmer working

Standing with and for others,
"We won't let any of our peers get corrupted"

Blindfold Unfolding

Monologues or dialogues
Dichotomous or polymorphic
1, 2, 3
Quadrupel the emphasis or cube it

The math origins are there for measurements
But my oh my
Is the soul worth anything?

They'll scratch their heads and look puzzled
She's got a point, is it qualitative?
Or infinite

How can anyone pull that off?
We practically cut you off
Who owns the funding now, who?
Who has the creative juice that keeps getting stolen?

-winks and smiles-

Do you want to keep lying and projecting?
Withhold opportunities
Depriving the commonwealth
Taking their intellectual property when you have trade secrets

You've got no time left, i'm telling you
She gave you warnings when she showed up going the distance to your cities

Better bake bread and goods
The plot twist is about to happen
With sweet cinnamon

39 - FARAH ALQATTAN

Honorable Gentle-Men

Where is faith, is it adversaries or unity?
The truth is abound fulfilling this life's mystery

They can tug at your mental operations so you can operate in
The function that can scare the ones beside you
Suggestions with subliminals

But flick that light on
Ouf
What's up with all that deception, a filth

Wisemen are you grown?
Perhaps mature
The glory, sure I guess
Byproduct
It won't upset them off for long
Because they'll learn not to judge a book by it's cover

Sweet Macaroons

Have you felt strong winds?
That pushed you back almost to your origins

If you find yourself there
Don't be frightened

Sit on your knee like a warrior or a gladiator
Scoop the dirt or dust
In the palm of your hands speaking,

"Thank you, I'll be who I'm meant to.
I'll answer my calling, without hesitation."

We may be dust, as skin sheds an ounce
But our origins are true
Rising even when we're breaking , beyond barriers

If you feel the wind
Don't be scared or scarred
Remember Pocahontas, felt spirit design
Lifting, "Colors of the wind"
With time, giving an attire more honorable

Perceive where is her soul essence now
Womanhood franchise
For those who shutout the warrior when she was fighting their battles
If they could, they'd want to keep others seeing her unworthy

So don't feel lonely, if you're amidst any suffering
Journal in your diary to share the glimpses of what's occurring
The documentation of evidence gathering
When they embed guilt in your consciousness
And tell you it'll be a final judgment in court heaven

Who will rule or advocate for you?
If not a true womanhood, protecting her household

This is spicy, it's known
But women need to be recognized for their strength
So true men see past their skin
Leading with kindness
Is it mother, wife, or daughter?
Who may have been taken advantage of

Don't let the anger surface
Pour in your cup empathy and compassion

Cortex Cortisol

Eyes will have sight
To see people into becoming more honorable

Even they who misbehaved
This is a carved opportunity

It's possible to put the past behind us and forgive
Write a new legacy for humanity

It takes accountability, to feel the hurt that has been hurting the body
How long has it been happening?
Perhaps generations

Why are none of you in compassion?
Or is resentment and contempt going to define us
Leading to more anguish disasters
It's important to distinguish

How many times is it going to take?
For her to turn the other cheek, reminding

"Love is powerful"

Stoic Enigma

*The dirty yards can give spots
And others look, to not see any treasures*

*But who feels the water?
Weighing the variables
Frequency vibration
Wiping their own eyes, from witnessing what's happening to man-kind*

*Hardly any try to take accountability
Emotions surface first, clouding reason
The prime impulse to constantly be blaming
Rather than empathizing
Maybe it's better to have more prisons*

All needing solitude rather than associative connections who are subdued

*How long will oppression last?
Rather than beautiful beauty mark impressions
That cover others with sacredness*

*If this is not love devotions
What is?
A heart, that refuses to give up on others even through the hardship*

Fortress Faith

Your name protects you
Don't change it even if you get offers to

What happens if you don't change yourself?
It pisses off those who don't want you to stay authentic

Even when you're feeling changes and elevations
Physiologically a whirlwind

Why let anyone re-define?
Don't they know, you've been loved since the day you were born?

You are not at fault for what's happening
Even when you've made mistakes
You are okay
Turn the harmful away

Practice majesty
And abstain from the scandalous
Even when they popularize it

If only you knew how much this author wants to cover the innocent
Who roamed through, because they've only lived in America
What is their point of reference?

Who has empathy? Who?
To understand even the son of anyone can be given a second chance

Keep the soul intact
Than operating believing false narratives or objects
There is a worse sin they said
So let this free you from worshiping anything
Especially people

You've been loved unconditionally
Protected from the beginning
It takes some time to gain awareness

Even the little kids repeat their mistakes
A pattern we were always meant to change
It takes maturity

So beauty, know you are more worthy than influential operation
If I could, I'd break marketing apart that keeps targeting after you
Exploiting insecurities

-sighs-

Oh the sunshine is bright
Don't let goodness be covered by the clouded

This author won't have it,
Gives it right back
"Won't bow down to liars or cowardice"

Beautiful and Unshaken

Boy oh Boy
Is that a girl?
Who does she think she is?
Writing and scaling different
Not yelling at others, putting up defenses

"Men know better,
They're the head of a household"
Sure, it's true
Until you perceive, some have grown up without fathers

The last is coming up
Or is it wisdom
Womanhood beaming through, speaking for generations

The soul is eternal, oh how it shines
She will too
Are we not one?

Deserving, beyond who can't perceive the modesty
Truth
Held in high honor and regard
Yes, she is
She won't need your permission to make changes, building temples

Or is it required to get a permit and a license
Bribes full of corruption
When they try to control your funding

Jokes on the fools
True fortune needs no permission
If you can perceive it
Who is really fighting for freedom?

Thinking true authority can be bought
When women who have wells of fortunes, sitting on the right side
Pouring instead of poisoning

"Feisty, these women are.
Why won't you control her?"
I know, isn't she priceless and not possessed?

Who has power? Now tell me who?
If not womanhood who builds fortress
Baring the children
While they cried, she awakened
Rocking you back and forth until you felt soothing

Perhaps even the men when they're older
Going home, to get warm cuddles

-smiles-

Who is tapped into source full of intuition
Not saying she is better than, pay her respect
Even if you have nothing in your pocket
Rather than making fun of her belongings

Gold Mine

When you love something, you'll fight for it
So here is this author, in the battle of her life, winning the war for humanity

Love never gives up
On anyone
Especially those who have been harmed because of deeper layers

Even with distance and time
When things are replaced or taken away
Love never gives up
Even when, the answer, requires to let go

High distinctions
Who propels not aiming to sink others

Never give up
No not in the heart or soul
You'll notice the power pouring into you

Love looks past the obvious to see deeper layers
In the details

Love not only stands firm when required
Humble enough to kneel in kindness
Even reaching as it's soaring
Because it knows it wouldn't have made it without the ones before it

Love is part of reason and purpose
Not in selfish desire but intentions

Love is compassion in the hardest times
Because it knows what it's like to feel broken

Love won't' close up, but opens a window, to let the light in
Is that fresh air you're breathing?

You've got a choice to make, everyday
A new beginning

Know, love will be with you and all around you, as some have chosen
Like this guardian

You can decide to be anything when the time comes
If you want to be the best,
aim to be honest

Love's power won't lie
When it stands up against injustice
It's garment isn't greedy

*It's a beauty to **be.long** in the beyond*
With time, you'll know

Connective Patent

What a masterpiece
A work of art
Or is it science
A lot bit of soul expression

This author is weaving through the fabric
Pivoting and doing different
Not for herself
But the longevity of what will become of us

She sees others running and at times in groups
She speaks, "I hope you spend your days running to and not from something"

So, if you go the distance
Like she has
You too, will be more than okay
Raising standards
Because you've got heart and a soul shining

Feel empowered!

Alternate function
Aim for progress
See yourself rising
And pretty soon the whole franchise
Not just womanhood but also brothers

It's beautiful when we learn to forgive each other
Up-skill and not kill
All the goodness that has been born from the beginning

<u>Musky Timber</u>

A lot can happen in a short instance
These miracles full of wonders
Some won't believe it until it materializes
So check your hands, what are you holding?

Don't fear, as this love sets you free
It's been by your side this whole time

While some buy their time, even bite their tongues
The lovely pours into cups
Is it love or a disaster
Perhaps, it's the true fortune

Can you read?
Between the lines and the rhymes
The power of love
Connecting the dots and state lines
Even countries across oceans

Making a populous blossom in heart and soul
Womanhood franchise, doing the impossible

Visual Spectrum

This one is going to standout
If you can perceive
Through the darkness
Is it a book or a person?

An unfolding, as it was written
Or is it better to be prejudice?

Strap in, we're taking off again
Who is going to save this galaxy?

If not for the guardians
A girl or a woman
A mother or a grandma
Womanhood franchise

The men too
All of us lifting one another either physically or in spirit
Inclusion

Easy Breezy, Lemon Squeezy

They teach you so many skills since you've been young
They are all required
Either what to do or refrain from
So keep an open mind and raise your awareness

You're a sponge absorbing all the intel
Then the epiphany happens
"Sponges can clean things up"
So lets see who's going to be shinning

Is it Kung Fu or a mic drop?
Better than the pills they sell for symptoms
Instead of empowering you to address the root cause infection

The landscape is present
As you walk through different cities
But what is it like without separations?
Is the body groaning from vices?

Even the bacterial infection when it has gone too long
The nerve needs to come out
Maybe it's a stand up
A comedy
To break it down, not each other for profit

-smiles-

Why need pharmaceuticals when there is a sunroom?
That keeps shinning

Is it dopamine or serotonin?
Thank god for all the nurses healing
In the attire or intelligence

Recognition Ignition

This author didn't want to take it this far
But they really asked for it

Was it men?
Or someone is getting a taste of their medicine
Perhaps it's iron sharpens iron

Let me be clear
They probed and picked, even insulted
Would you rather anyone continue to be silent?
Unsympathetic or empathetic to their kindred
Womanhood

Or did you think she wasn't going to stand up for others?
Sisters and brothers

Perhaps, reflecting the virtue of loyalty
Oh my
A woman leading as an example
Setting the standards
Without weapons
Perhaps we need people to vote for her
For anyone to recognize her for her worth

But if they knew the power of words
They would have stayed silent
Or would they rather face a global uprising?

Do those entities get any criticisms
Law suits or plea deals
Not taking accountability
Yet women are scrutinized for what they're not covering
When algorithms are popularizing the trending and suggesting the enticement
Are you ready to face the making?

Diamond Wings

Each will have to overcome
Hurdles

Why keep focused on the minorities and the reports
Instead of the overcoming, soon no one will be struggling

So what is each facing?
Violence or abandonment
Ignorance or greed
Mate, even anxiety

Why do we focus on the labels?
Rather than the hurdle
To lift rather than judge
Cultivating empathy is important

Womanhood is sacred and will be covered
Either in spirit or the physical
When they're selling everything cropped at stores

Who judges others for what they wear?
Either in function or attire

Let's focus on the patterns
Is it statistics or data science
If you're the least bit aware
You would have noticed the lesson
Correlation does not mean causation
Perhaps risk management
When everyone needed to learn abstinence

No Strings Attached

It's getting juicy isn't?
When they're waiting for you to self incriminate
How will they hold this against you
Or above you

No worries, it's clarity
Experience is meant to elevate
Or is she going to keep getting called an alchemist

More labels, when language was created to uplift
Given clues, through generations
If you had an inkling to study
Learn the origins of Arabic
Instead of criticizing

Perhaps learning about physiology can help
Open the heart to understand stimulants and inhibitors

Even America saved this authors life, time and time again
When her home country was being chemical weapon threatened
While her family had to board up their house
Like they do in hurricane seasons

So are we going to keep hating?
Each other and leaders?
Those honorable men who made hard decisions
Now seeing the dividends, of their past choices

May peace and love be poured from her
In it the infrastructure or mental temples
Connective

Foreigners rising to help
Or is it womanhood franchise
With fresh understanding
So none fall to bias, to start overgeneralizing

FARAH ALQATTAN

Lady Liberty

Is it true luxury you're after?
Or the capital gains stored up in plastics
Maybe digital servers

She's been the best net worth you can ever have
Who has taken care of you?

For better or worse
For richer or poorer
In sickness and in health
To love and to cherish
Until death.. even after
Is this a proposal?

Perhaps, it's just a reminding of origins
That of love and forgiveness
Putting first things first, instead of profit
Humanity overcoming a hurdle

Is it violence or abuse
Mutilation of body parts to be bigger
Rather than acceptance
Objectifying
When they're all glowing in soul essence

So renew your vows, in how you carry yourself
Even if you're not married... yet

Hope Happenings

Forgiveness maybe the hardest act
In this story breaking chains

When you forgive it frees
Not only yourself but also generations

It's easy to absorb the pain and sit on it
Keep sitting there in the mental and physical
Next thing you know, decades have passed you
Talking like a broken record

But this here will move you different
Frees you without weapons

Are we ready for a new experience?
That won't hurt in the name of anything or anyone?

Can we even handle it?
Peacefulness
Not the chaos and destruction we've become accustomed to
Even gossip

Who made a lens?
Rather than free focus
To shift perception from what is, to what they deemed was important
Shifting understanding
Instead of evaluating, root cause manifestations

This author can give more clues
But perhaps, it's better to keep it open ended
Rather than have you locked in perception
Empowering you to critically think

Don't be an over-thinker, until you twinkle
So if that light comes on
This has served it's purpose, sparking your genius

The genius isn't one who thinks they're the smartest, full of arrogance
It's one who realizes they actually know so little, even when they gather
At times, being patient through others development
Even with the dark energy
Requiring purity

Acknowledgment too is important
Than denial full of deflections
Leading to willful blindness
It's best to gain awareness
To understand sense of expressions

"Wait, what was this about?"

Hope happenings

63 - FARAH ALQATTAN

Lily Pond

Genetics defines in pairs
X and Y chromosomes
And developers, pointing to axis points

Mathematics
To realize there are decimals and duodecimals
Giving the same outcomes
Except one is better applicable

What about technology?
1's and 0's can equal to 77
Lighthouse forgiveness

This isn't logical
There's even imaginary numbers
Rationals too
So if the math ain't mathin'
Start subtracting

"Where is this leading?"

Perhaps getting you comfortable in ambiguity
Not feeling dumb or like a genius
Humble to learn engineering

Is it shuttles or ships?
Software building pyramids
Is it a simulation?
Or things unseen, maybe an Egyptian origin

The hope and the love worth more than anything

How can anyone quantify?
What can be poured from the heart and soul
While some think she's worthless because she hasn't given what they expected

Do you want to measure it?
Perhaps the waist size is better to grip

Can we aim to be intelligent or wise?
To know, womanhood franchise is perils

With time, she can look you in the eye
Either send you daggers or soft elevations
Without even using weapons

-winks-

What a flow
That is not logical at all

But even the movies showcased
She speaks her own language
Better to get educated

Or is the lesson having to repeat itself?
Through generations
Final test

Here's a hint
Here's a clue
Oh wait, I think you said you'd prefer to do it alone
Without inclusion

Virtue Exfoliation

How can one grow to be standing on their own?
If it wasn't for the help of the unseen
To be able to perceive
How faith carried humanity
Womanhood advocating for her neighbors and children

"Women are too emotional for leadership"
Think again, the eyes can only see a sliver of the spectrum
Or are they going to keep diagnosing
Throwing labels on the disability list
Instead of weighing soul oppression

How aware is each to understand
Physical bodies don't have eyes behind their heads
To keep looking and making assumptions
Even belittle others, perhaps womanhood

Or will women too grow humble
Not to gossip on one another

Yes, this checks the men and puts them in their place
A requirement

Women too have to grow to be accountable

It wouldn't be fair for them to not continue to lead
You know what I mean?

-smiles-

Elemental Productions

Nothing new is under the sun
Others will say "Everything you ever wanted to invent is already been done"

But who delivers?
Sequences

What is your belief system in?
Who is guiding or stealing from it?
Does it have hopefulness?

Not weighing the patterns
Since everyone goes about conforming, leading to the same outcomes

Perhaps there's nothing new
As one grows old
Having consumed all the recipes

It seems so sad, doesn't it
To not believe in our happy ending
Diverse unity

Look here this offering
A new opportunity, to start believing
To experience newness
Or will it take revitalization?

Are you still full of joy?
Or feeling dull because of routines?

The impossible is being made possible
With time, chains will be breaking
That oppression no longer existing

Or are we going to think harm will rule us
Not giving womanhood an opportunity
To have this populous blossoming

Is it an uprising?
No, no, no
None will revolt or get violent anymore
Only sitting in stillness experiencing heaven 'us'
Time will tell

It's in the details, ain't it
Or are these seeds going to go to waste?

Perhaps we can start plucking those weeds
That were implanted
Is it a chip?

Unified Faction

There are so many
Honorable Men

As some might not be able to observe
How they treat their kindred
Covering them even in private discussions

There is high honor, here
Of men who show up doing the great things

Ones who bare the cold and storms
Preparing shelters and responding to disasters

Men who wheel others into health to make sure others are healed
Even gardening picking up litter

There are so many who move with respect and dignity
Saying, "Excuse me or pardon"
Not hesitating to witness and validate the soft eyes before them, that have been crying
Even when it's emotional and not logical

Women, you are fortune
Give men their due respect as well
At times, you may not see what they've had to tolerate
They're worthy of gratitude

We can lead so different
Looking out for one another
Being gentle

Caring too
Making a fresh meal
That isn't only spicy but sweet

Even this author had a stranger, she was taught to call uncle
Who stepped in to teach driving lessons
While others could perceive, there was no father figure
That Chevy Impala getting a couple of bumps
Instead of lashing out, he smiled and looked speaking "Everything is all right, keep going"

There are others who step up in ways unseen
Doing kind things
Sharing
Kindness

It's important to see and value the whole picture
Take time to recall the goodness
So the bitterness doesn't take shape
Manifesting in hurtful behavior

Catalyst Conduit

*Gratitude for each other
Is a compass to compassion*

*Even as shown on screens
Attempts to bend the fabric of physics
For rights rather than responsibility*

*Women have been at fault too
Doing wrong acts in sensations
Even this author is willing to acknowledge it
It's better to be accountable, even if it gets you hated*

*Women have had their ways too
Doing things not so honorable
As development takes time
Spurs of graces*

*So what can each do?
Keep pointing the finger not being accountable
Yelling and shouting
While others are watching*

*How many still need us?
In spirit and behavior
Carrying ourselves different
Rather than getting accustomed to selfishness*

*If you weigh the variables
Of why you've felt hurt or harmed
And reflect on how each carried themselves
It wont take long
To realize
We can all be doing better*

Energy Vibrations

As this stays objective
It'll be easier to digest
Rather than subjectivity
That can lure into misinterpreting

Who's at fault really?
Is it mental mechanisms?
Or reflection of operations
Perhaps a growing learning

Empowerment is important
Rather than anything that can make any feel helpless

Be empowered, you can be great
Not over anyone but former self
Rather than blaming others

Gracious Discretion

It's vital
To shift in sight
Identifying insights

Can each shift through the lenses
To be able to witness
Not only the good
But the flaws
So each can see appropriately
Choosing to be better

Why do we need each other?
Even the haters
They're expressing what's required
Objective awareness

Everyone is appreciated here
So don't look down on anyone without value

Some could be behaving
Aim to seek understanding

Practically everyone would need to focus on the harmful
And the negative things
To be able to untether
Not wanting

After sometime, reflecting
Was it really the right direction?
If not founded in gratitude
Leading to resentment roots

Bright Future

Faith is a word
It's a name
Often mistaken with religion

Faith can be an armor
or fuel
Sustenance on a silver platter
Giving clues

Faith won't distress
Easily empowers
Looking beside, helping ·
Full of fortune

Faith seeks higher aims
Progress
Leading to bright futures

Is it men or women called faith?
Perhaps the intelligence is coded

Factorial

Words identify
They can shape shift perception
In a good way or hurting

Words can lead to better outcomes
Carving kindness
Instead of attacking

Words can be complex mixed with emotions
When they surface explaining the occurrences

Words can be true or false
Requiring awareness
To digest the message

The teachers spent so many days giving materials
Then tested to weigh if any were paying attention
After giving the passage

Is this question true or false
Is her love worth anything at all?

Fertile Integrity

There are objects and energies present
Carrying specific directions

Some can take one way high
Others can have one going on a merry go round

Some clean and clear
And can be used for good

Other times, things are inherited
In behaviors

What about the effect?
Domino's rippling

Womanhood or men
Perhaps this is drawing attention to the children mirroring

Star Spangled Banner

Who rejects truth
And decides to abide in lies

Who experiences that weight of secrecy
Negligence
To understand the power of care, lifting and empowering

Dressing up
Any wounds from the hurts

Wiping any tears
With grace, whispering
"You are more than you can possibly know.
Aim to seek higher guidance and wisdom."

Keep reaching
Be touched
Without anyone taking your clothes off
Violating the best parts about you
Without grip
This love is gentle

How can any learn how to be
If they have not experienced
The kind and caring
To return a better investment

This love won't give up
The fight has just been won
So celebrate this offering
Lifting to a better future
Inclusion, with womanhood

Who would consciously keep harming
Acting like the soul is to be sold, for profit
After this has been given

If they ignore it
They'll know what will be written for them
Was it not said
Who truly would know you to the depths?
In heart and soul
Giving fortunes

How long will we ignore one another
Looking not seeing goodness
When it has been poured from day 1

"Womanhood, we're so sorry.
For belittling you before you even made it to this planet."

Good thing her worth was written on her heart
Before she even arrived
Or else it would have been better for her to be kept caged
Under false opinions and statements
Spells of utterances
Or do tongues need to be silenced?

Mountain Peak

How did we get here?
How did we climb?
If it wasn't for the harm that now has made each shine

How can we share gratitude
For the tough time
And the rhymes
And the light that still beams standing alone

How is it even powered up?
Electricity or soulfulness

What abides all around and within
The heart beats faster when it's soul essence
Sharing and reading
Knowing
This is the true fortune

Step Up

Get those shoes ready
That armor
Perhaps more than any material, choosing radiance

Women
Men
Are you ready?

To be kind and gentle to one another
Expression
Without regression
or the depression from senselessness

How can each be accountable
Owning more than property but actions
To carry oneself in attire
With a kind glow and radiance

Can we look past the physical
Experience the beyond

A better response-able belonging

Orange Tangerines

This fruit
Is it ripe?
Sweet
Perhaps you'll notice how subjectivity really manifests

How is it that we can agree on anything
If we do not go beyond the senses?

Are you still gripping?
Hand in hand
Taking you to experience wholesomeness
One essence

Uncover
Discover

Don't turn your back on the beauty of the unshaken
Beaming inside 'us'

Every act in love
Can turn the darkest times
To a new dawn horizon

True love will never have you forget
How much beauty resides in each of us
So perhaps this is humors
To help you differentiate
Fruit Fruit Fruit
Who is ripe and sweet
Oozing with goodness and not greed

Beyond Enduring, Endearing

Man oh Man
How come?
Little things make a difference

Man oh Man
How come?
Her intention sets new precedents

Man oh Man
How come?
A womanhood franchise being modest and accountable

Man oh Man
How come?
All on her own, who is really standing beside her

Man oh Man
How come?
Perceive true guidance

Man oh Man
How come?
Womanhood, climbing helping her neighbors

Man oh Man
How come?
The impossibilities of deliverance
Without birth pains
Newborns
Or a celebration
For a new life we can reside in
Each being becoming
A true one

Or has the soul always been there?
Hidden beyond world reflections
Is this an uncovering
To have you see glimpses of the fortune

Don't take her for granted

Look around
And see within
How true fortune, has always been right beside you
Cheering for you to win

Do you see her iris?
Of what resides within her?
Even this is empowering her to see her own worth

How come?
Have any possibly forgotten
Who really is the golden child
Glowing in radiance
All generations

<u>Tennis Love</u>

*They say god gives everyone a gift
But perhaps each will need to answer their call to spark it into becoming*

Moving across the terrain and energy vibrations

*Who will be able to withstand?
The attacks and the insults
The beat downs and poisons
Even the insights flooding in consciousness raising awareness
While they lose the one's they love beside them
Still walking in faithfulness
Not knowing, what's on the other side
And the direction keeps tugging for them to keep moving forward*

*How can we leave a footprint?
In the snow or soil
Being a guide
Do we need to be giants?*

*Better than a hand imprint
On anyone's cheek
Leaving bruises and markings
Choosing to rise as heroines*

*So if you find this
Take your step
Higher elevation
In kindness*

There are many who have existed
Leaving a trail
To a love and happy ever after
Not growing to be impulsive

Don't fear
We are all growing here
So give grace to the development of others near
While choosing to be sincere
To those you see

Yes, women too
Pouring kindness from within them
To share with their kindred
Here, take your well of fortune

Did you think your inheritance would just be materialistic?

We can learn to force others into doing
At times, opting for more prisons

Or we can lean into higher powers
Inspiration and kindness
Reminding
Of responsible behaviors

So reach in
Find a heart of courage

Sometimes, all we need is a mirror
Not one reflecting physically
But soul essence
Permanence
Unshaken beauty character
Perhaps with time, it'll make a better profit

Together

How many can you lean on out here?
With trust, faith, and loyalty

Take this power and feel transcendence
Not looking into the camera, popularizing trends
Amplify robotics
Are we going to end up in the matrix?

Perhaps there's one planting
A paradise, happy after

Is it women, planting gardens?
In the open fields
Or the temple

Womanhood looking out for one another
A covering
No longer insulting

This entire book isn't against anyone, really
It's empowering each with fuel to choose different
Launch you out of the harm or hurting

There's been so many who have remained true
Admitting truths
Understanding even the best fall sometimes
This soil can be softened
Ozzing with forgiveness

"It's getting repetitive"

That's the goal
So we're not preemptively attacking

Yes, reach for understanding

-smiles, gripping hand-

What are you still holding onto?
Resentment or love
Discern the difference
Growing awareness

Withdrawal Reflex

How did you wake up?
Was it abrupt or gentle?

Can things be smooth
Even nature has perks

Perhaps this is shaking you
Not so hard, gentle
To be able to notice
The compounding effect, beyond physical perception

How much time have each spent?
Sitting out of the office noticing the cycles
Not just the water but the attires
Instead of leaning on predictive functions

Better lean into higher intelligence
Or would you rather keep insulting the making?
Through innovation

Have you noticed how each moves about?
Different age groups, races, and zip codes

How many are for equity?
Perceiving the one who works leaves to drive through
Higher pressure
Or is it blood
Look through the heart lens
You'll grow with compassion

Sweet Pressure

Did any think others don't notice
Witness
Not in judgment, prejudice, or bias

Whats the difference?
In all of us if we're all the same
Perhaps how one challenges themselves and others to grow objective

Some may say, it's not possible
"How can one be objective, when they can't hear what's going on in the amazonian?"

Objectivity isn't physical
If one perceives
Humble enough to witness
Parking their sense of self

While you've read this
Lets ask, "How many times did subjective opinions surface?"
Disagreements or Arguments

Where was that learned?
Lawyers and the bylaws
How long have we been fighting instead of observing
Bypassing
All the clues given by consciousness

Perhaps it takes women to be intuitive
Help her colleagues to understand the difference
To rise up civilization than devour it

"Is it possible?
Humanity can be flourishing"

The irony, even with this
Conscience will surface answers

Or is it ego?
Are you wanting to be right or feel transcendence?

Same same but different

-smiles-

Covered Goodness

Soft but sweet
Tender
Breeze

Windy, how is she?
Has she been kind, serving
Putting a plate of food on a table
Perhaps baking

How about Olivia?
Silky sweet smooth attire

Even Rose
Vibrant

Victory Victoria
Divine Diana

Even Joy
Through experience so many shine brightly

How important is each?
Without materials exuding fortunes
Perhaps it's in the making or naming
Better upgrade your vocabulary

Are you able to perceive or see?
Algorithms won't be able decode the genes
Higher intelligence
Rather than biased decisions

Score

Divide
Split apart
Is it meiosis?
Seperation
Making or giving more production

How will others act now?
After reading a little glimpse of heaven

Will others go about insulting
Not giving but hoarding

How much has been given to you?
Without materials
In foundation

So if nothing was added here's this
Generosity
Giving love without the need for profit

How priceless is the best
Giving you a whole lot of fortune without embedding fear in consciousness

Did you unlock the mystery yet?
Here is the box

No, no
Have you only been conditioned to think it would be a ring or Santa Claus?

Perhaps its something different than a phrase
A passage reminding to be kind to womanhood
Since they can be beautifully creative

Rather than being fixed in the box to logistic operations
Wait, no, it's the twentieth century dealing with a black coded ruling
Algorithms
Artificial Intelligence

Or is any prepared to eat
From the organic sacred origins
Instead of propagating the harming
Then blaming others for sinning

Look now, so deep
Is it the iris of another or your own doing

Lady Justice

"They're setting you up"
Thank you very much

"You'll have no funding"
Look who has fortunes

"You'll be homeless"
Where? Here?
In the house of the royal

"You don't have enough experience"
Yet, wisdom keeps pouring.
While they charge towards the wrong direction.
Not heeding

"You don't belong, go back to where you came from"
Really, do you want to experience another new precedent.
Lobbying full of moral turpitude
Without the presumption of innocence
If it's recalled, its part of the constitution

"She won't make it on her own, she's not strong enough"
Are you really awaiting for others to falter?
Not reflecting on your inner mirror
Naysers

Perhaps, being proactive can serve a better purpose
Eat up
Prayer and meditation
Seeking higher guidance

Then witness as her angels show up
Not just for her but humanity as well

Come on now
Don't frown
Keep your chin up
These hands have always been gentle
Even to the oppressors

Is it the sun, stars, or moon do you see?
Glowing
Heavenly ones leading

Or is it still about genders?
Still needing to get over that hurdle
When men and women were created equal

-smiles-

Mark 6:11
Matthew 10:14

Matthew 7:6

Book soundtrack:
Kick the Dust - Ryan Taubert

About the Author

Farah Alqattan migrated to the United States, along with her family in 2000 from the middle-east. While developing in various cities, Farah was able to successfully complete her Bachelor of Arts in Criminal Justice and Master of Science in Cybersecurity.

In 2019, Farah recognized various patterns occurring through the interdependence of operations in space leading to outcomes. In an effort to contribute proactively, Farah spent her recent years sharing writings founded from unseen guidance, aimed to raise awareness. She has grown to be multi-strategic, with a career focus on AI governance, while sharing creative proposals and projects for building a better future. She's been able to persevere through trials by focusing on peacefulness, love, and meditation. In revelatory time, she developed a new motto, "Better you, better we!" and shifted to utilize her social media platform for social responsibility purposes; featuring 'Operation Uplift, Tip Bits'.

Ultimately, Farah knows all this is likely a manifestation of her prayers being answered to heal the soul of a nation. Recognizing that miracles really are possible, should we keep our hearts open to receiving them while taking inspired actions. We hope you've enjoyed this publication and invite you to review her other poetry book collection 'To you From you', packing more gifted goodness.

About the Publisher

Rwh Publishing LLC was established in 2023 to publish creative content by artists that aim to uplift humanity and change lives for the better. Thank you for your support, in building a better future.